BIG SISTER LEARNS

ALL ABOUT BABIES ⁴

Best buddies
(9–18 months)

WRITTEN BY POLLY ZIELONKA

ILLUSTRATED BY MARIA KIRSHINA

Dedication

The first baby of the family, Dude:

You are one of a kind – moving around the world,

making friends everywhere you go, and being so patient with two babies

coming along. We all love you so much.

Claire's baby brother, Eddie, is not so tiny anymore.
He's getting big, but he is still a baby.

He still needs lots of milk, and cuddles.

Eddie is getting to be very playful,
and he is crawling everywhere.

He also waves,

and claps

and loves to dance!

Eddie really wants to walk and run, just like Claire. He pulls himself up to stand, and takes a few steps!

Oops! He fell down.
"Good job, Eddie!" Claire exclaims.

Learning to walk takes a lot of practice.
They watch him carefully, and Claire
cheers him on.

Eddie is also making a lot of new sounds and babbles to Claire. She listens and plays along, even when she's not sure what he's saying.

"Wow, Eddie. What else happened?"

"Eeeeeee!!!!!" Eddie squeals!

"That is too loud for my ears!"
Claire complains.

Eddie is discovering how to
use his voice. But sometimes
it's a bit too noisy.

Claire and her mommy show him how to whisper instead,
"Eddie, can you whisper like this?"

He stops to listen. Then he babbles, "ba ba ba."
He is not whispering yet, but he is much quieter.

"Here you go, Eddie. Now it's your turn."
Claire rolls a ball to Eddie.

Then she holds out her hands,
"can you roll it back to me, Eddie?"

Claire is teaching Eddie how to share and take turns.
He does not always give toys back to her,
but he is getting much better.

Sometimes Claire needs a bit of help with Eddie.
She's trying to build a sand castle, and
he's trying to knock it down.

"Okay Eddie, let's build something else to knock down,"
her mommy tells him.

"Here, you can use this," Claire hands him a shovel.
"Oh, thank you!" says Claire's mommy.

When they get home, they turn on their favorite music for a dance party.

"Awe, Dude came to watch! See, Eddie,
we pet him gently like this."

Claire and Eddie are learning a lot of new things together.
And they have become best buddies.

Printed in Germany
by Amazon Distribution
GmbH, Leipzig